Contents

22/10/2020

I stopped listening

It was easier to tune into the voices I could hear

Than those I could not

Including my own

Buried under the layers of external conditioning

Stories upon stories added

So, to hear my own voice

I needed to start digging

It seemed easy at first

Yet as time went on

I thought I've got this

I don't need to listen

To myself anymore

The volume turned up

On those around me

Listening to what they were telling me

Their prophecies

Their truths

Their knowing

Yet I had stopped

I stopped listening

To my voice

To my truth

To my knowing

And in doing so

I lost myself

Foreword

When I started writing this book, I wasn't 100% sure what it was going to be about. A continuation of my journey? My channelings received through meditation? My learnings from living in a caravan? It has become a combination of everything above and maybe more. As I began to edit this book, I realised I had so much more that I wanted to share, so I have scoured all of my notebooks and notes that I have made in the last year and a bit to bring you not only practical tips but also, hopefully, some words of inspiration as we shift into this new era which is where we are.

To be at the cusp of a changing civilisation feels exciting and scary all at once. Yet, here we are. For those of us brave enough, I see you, for those ready to take the leap, I see you, for those wanting to, I see you. Here's to us, to our future and to our children's futures. I have included my own forage into foraging and growing. I used to tell myself I couldn't grow anything but that story seems to be dissolving as I clear a patch of land and, with the help of my kids, begin to grow herbs and vegetables. A special thank you to my neighbour, Pauline, who listened to me when I said I wanted to create a vegetable garden and has helped me turn my ideas into a reality.

At this time, many of us have become disillusioned with society as we know and have known it. For those of us born in the 1980s, we have seen the rise of materialism and consumerism yet there is still this yearning to go back to a simpler life and now this yearning is growing into something much more. It is becoming many people's dreams and is in many people's visions. I can see us eventually moving into creating offgrid communities around the world.

Patience is a must as we begin to explore these new territories in an en masse venture into the unknown. We are in a time of creating new structures and systems that will work for us not against us.

I hope that, within these pages, you find something that will help you in your offgrid journey - whether it is a line that jumps out at you, a practical tip to follow or inspiration that if I can do this shizz, so can you!

Acknowledgements

There are so many people that I want to thank for their continued love and support in allowing me to be me and live my crazy ass dreams.

To my parents for never judging me or questioning my decisions, allowing me space to evolve and grow as the soul I am.

To my sister for keeping me grounded, as always.

To my children for choosing to come on this journey with me, which I remind them of often.

To my friends, Claire, Dave, David, Pauline and Kate who all believed that I could do this, have supported me through this transition and continue to do so.

To the many people who have contacted me regarding their own offgrid journey, and shared their experiences and wisdom, I thank you.

To the souls who have come into my life for a reason, season or lifetime, thank you. We are all connected in this Universe.

To everyone who is choosing to read this book, I thank you.

To those who inspire me on a daily basis thank you.

Lindsay x

The hues of pink and blues and whites

Shone above her

An alarm went off in the distance

The birds flapped

And tweeted in the air

The sound of sunset

Another day nearly over

Making the passing

Of new experiences and people

Where had this day gone?

How had it been spent?

Aware and in the moment?

Unaware and somewhere else?

The recognition that she had been

Where she was meant to

At every stage following her intuition

Conversations to be had

And energy to flow

Guided by herself and her alone

Feeling that freedom within

Not constrained by her own thoughts or beliefs

Or that of others

A childlike innocence

Whizzing on a zipwire

Flying through the air

Allowing herself within those moments to be free

Chapter 1 - The Introduction

I inadvertently found myself in a sweat lodge one evening and that is where this story begins.

It was the summer of 2018 and I had organised a social evening for members of my Facebook group, Consciousness Arising. We had been meeting up in a pub in York for a few months but the setting didn't really feel apt. A few days before our planned meet-up, a friend shared a post on Facebook saying that some Mexican Shamanic healers were staying at their healing centre and facilitating healing sessions. It was only a ten-minute drive away and I had already expressed my interest in going along. One of the members of the group, Paul, messaged me suggesting that we all meet at the healing centre instead of our usual pub. Awesome idea! Little did I know then that this was going to be one of those pivotal points in my life.

Twelve of us gathered in what felt like the middle of nowhere, a beautiful house in the middle of the countryside with an outdoor yurt, a fire and as close to nature and the outdoors as you can get.

We were greeted warmly by the owners of the healing centre, Nam Prakash and her son, Jote Prakash. We sat drinking herbal teas and chatting. Some of the members of the group went off to have some healing work. I think the session was maybe 45 minutes and then another group went. It must have been around 9pm by the time the healing sessions had finished.

When Nam Prakash asked if we wanted to stay to experience the sweat lodge, I shrugged my shoulders and was like, 'Yeah, why not?' Five others in the group also said yes. As we gathered in the kitchen for another cup of tea, I asked Nam Prakash what a sweat lodge actually was and what it entailed. She explained that we would all be going inside a hut that had been made the previous day; inside would be hot stones which water would be poured over and the hut would begin to heat up. We would also need to take our clothes off. I wasn't exactly prepared for this. I had stopped wearing a bra about three months before and the idea of getting in the hut with ten other men and women, semi-naked, wasn't something I was prepared for. Claire nearly spat her tea out as she exclaimed that she had just had her first herbal tea that evening and now she was going to be getting into a hut semi-naked! Thankfully, we were all given towels to cover our modesty. For those who haven't experienced a sweat lodge before, I will explain what the process was for us so that, if you ever find yourself in the same situation, at least you will feel prepared.

The beautiful Mexican Shamanic healer and his daughter had lit a fire close to the makeshift sweat lodge. We stood nearby offering prayers as he performed a beautiful ceremony under the Full Moon. I think we did this for around 30 minutes before being invited to remove most of our clothing. I remember trying to strip off in the darkness and trying to cover my boobs at the same time. Thankfully, I had my big pants on and not a tiny G-string as this would probably have been even more uncomfortable. With the aforesaid towel wrapped around me, I and the other women were invited into the space first. As we bent down and entered the darkness, we found that there wasn't enough room to stand. Inside the centre of the space was a pile of stones. We made our way clockwise around the circle and crouched down to take our spaces. Sitting on mud and twigs, I could feel branches poking through my towel and tried to make myself as comfortable as possible. There were a few giggles as we tried to get comfortable and people got twigs in places they hadn't had twigs before. Thankfully, we couldn't see very much so the towel protected my modesty.

As we sat in a circle, more prayers were offered to ancestors and our Mexican Shaman began chanting. Hot water was brought in to be poured on the stones and soon hints of eucalyptus and other beautiful herbs began to enter my sinuses. It was refreshing and cleansing. As the sweat began to pour from my brow, I entered into a fairly deep meditative state. I had no idea how long we were going to be there for, so I settled into it. At one point, I remember feeling mentally uncomfortable as I wasn't used to being in one space for such a long time. Suddenly, in my mind's eye, I saw my Native American guide. He stood beside me on the edge of a cliff. 'Claim the unclaimed land', he told me. What? As ever, my guide was cryptic and didn't give me any further information. I just remember thinking afterwards, 'What the fuck?' Why was my guide always so cryptic? What did this mean? I went home and googled it. Not much came up and I still wasn't fully aware of what it meant. As usual, the Universe decided to help me out.

One morning around 3am I woke up and, as I was not able to get back to sleep, I decided to once again google 'claiming the unclaimed land'. This time, I happened across a blog by The Small Farmer. It literally described the process of how to claim the unclaimed land. Unfortunately, juggling work and two children, I struggled to find the time to follow it up or pursue it.

During lockdown, I discovered a platform called Telegram and somehow stumbled across a group called the Offgrid Community Network UK. Lord knows how I found it but I did and I am so grateful. Kate Brown set up the group after hearing many people say they wanted to get out of 'the system'. By the way, Kate is now in the stages of setting up a community in Scotland after chatting with some of the members of the group. Pretty soon, I was attending meetings and offering to support North Yorkshire. I wasn't entirely sure what I was doing but it felt aligned and it was amazing to meet all these like-minded folk who wanted to go offgrid and live in communities in the UK. You can find the link to the group at the end of the book if you would like to join. I have also set up an Awakened Offgrid Community on Facebook for people to share ideas, to connect and to gather. Kate has been a huge inspiration to me as not only does she talk the talk, but she actually walks the walk. I know it's a huge cliché but when you see someone else taking action and making your dreams and visions a possibility, you feel more able to do it yourself.

If you are reading this and haven't heard of me before or seen the work I do, I will give you a brief background. My upbringing was fairly normal. My dad was a milkman and my mam worked for the Inland Revenue. I went to school, got my A Levels and headed to Mexico to teach English for four months. Applying to universities, I decided to do a degree in International Business. There were two reasons for this; one was that it was generic enough that I would be able to get a job easily when I graduated, or so I thought; the second was that I got a gap year in between and chose to study in Hong Kong. I was there in 2002 at the time of the SARS outbreak. All of the international students were flown home, except the Brits. The Halls of Residence was like a ghost town. Twelve of us left to fend for ourselves. It was here that I was first introduced to Reiki.

I graduated with a 2:2 and applied for jobs. Tesco was my 75th job application and I started working in Peterborough as a Health and Beauty/Homeshop Manager. Working there was stressful as you can imagine. It was the second biggest store in the UK at the time. I was drinking ten cups of coffee a day, smoking twenty cigarettes and the stress began to build up. At the time, I thought this was how life was. Working in a corporate environment, working long hours, feeling stressed, all part and parcel of life, right? A breakup with my boyfriend, reapplying for my own job and a house move left me fairly broken. I remembered Reiki so booked myself in for a session. To be honest, I thought it was a waste of money as I didn't feel anything at the time. However, I was intrigued so I went along to learn it. My life took a pivotal turn after this and I was drawn into a world of crystals, angels and mediumship.

I continued my retail path until 2010 when I left to set up my own business, NRG Healing, with my now ex-husband. I began giving Reiki sessions to people and hosting pamper evenings. I fell pregnant later that year so family life became paramount but I still read a ton of books about the afterlife and spiritual topics.

In 2016, my friend passed away, which was another pivotal moment. I realised that I had become emotionally numb to life. My marriage collapsed and I set up NRG Healing again as a way to earn some money whilst caring for my small children. Once again, I delved back into the spiritual world, opening myself up to my psychic and mediumistic abilities, meditating and following my intuition. Later, I would be drawn to shamanism, plant medicine and I began to do past life readings and enjoy my journey.

I am sharing this with you so that you know my background and that this way of living wasn't something I was born into. I had one caravan holiday in my late thirties with my kids and my parents up in Berwick. Even that didn't push me into this way of living. It has been a combination of listening to my intuition and feeling guided to be where I am now. It hasn't been without its challenges and life hasn't gone the way I thought it would but that is all part of our journey, right? I will talk about some of the challenges I have faced later in the book. However, for the most part, I have found myself in a community of like-minded people and my connection to nature and the outdoors has expanded. I began to work with the plants and nature around me and I have learned so much more than I ever did in school.

I took a leap of faith into the unknown and if I can do it, so can you.

Chapter 2- Declutter

In March 2020, lockdown came. I was sort of prepared for this as I had had a lot of communication from spiritual beings the year before. I just wasn't exactly sure of HOW things were going to change. As schools closed and businesses began to shut up shop, I realised this was it. This was the change that was necessary in order for us, as humans, to move forward and live in a more sustainable way. You can read more about the communication I was given in my book 'Voices from the Past, Present & Future; Insights into 2020 and Beyond'. I started home-schooling my children along with my ex-husband. He tends to do the Maths and English whilst I do the outdoors, nature, socialising, crafts and arts side.

Spending more time at home made me realise I was missing something. I was missing connection and purpose. I decided to make a start on decluttering my home. I had already Marie Kondo'd my house the year before but I was still shocked at how much 'stuff' I had. I am not going to lie - this wasn't an easy process and took several months. Not only is there the practical side of decluttering but it can also be quite emotional and bring up a lot of emotions for you. I talk you through this later on in the book.

Books

This was one of the most difficult items to give away. I have carried books around with me since I left home at nineteen. I have packed and unpacked boxes of books in over fifteen houses. I moved around a lot after I left home, moving every one or two years. I thanked my books for the wisdom they had imparted and the meaning they gave to me and then I packed them into boxes for the charity shop. My Famous Five collection went, all thirty of them, alongside books I had been saving for a rainy day, that I thought I would read again but never actually did. I realised that we accumulate books as a way to show off our wisdom and knowledge. I now have a small collection in my caravan but these are mostly reference books for plants, herbs and plant medicine. Any books that are fiction are read and then given to others. I now buy most of my books from charity shops and sometimes I am gifted books, for which I am always grateful.

Photos

I have been so lucky to have travelled quite extensively in my early twenties and, as such, I had taken lots of photos (before we could have them on our phones). However, the downside was that I had accumulated two huge boxes of photos. There were probably over 5000 photos in there. I went through each one and asked myself, do I need to keep this? Do I still have fond memories of me and this person? I went through the boxes with a glass of red wine, tearing them all up to burn. It took me about a week to go through all of them and then had a huge fire to release all my past memories. Sometimes, our photos may take us to painful places or times. These can go too as energetically you are saying, 'I am ready to let it all go'. When we begin to let go of 'stuff', we create new spaces for other 'stuff' to come in.

Paper documents

Many of us have probably held onto paperwork for

years 'just in case'. I used to file all my bills and keep a variety of papers that I never really needed so, again, I went through all of my paperwork and burned what I no longer needed. What I did need, I kept in a small folder to put into storage.

Clothes

Having a practical wardrobe whilst living offgrid is essential and yet there is also room for beautiful dresses. What I will say about all those clothes you have been keeping 'just in case' is, get rid. I now have a summer and winter wardrobe and not much in between; a pair of sturdy walking boots, wellies and Birkenstocks, for as soon as the sunshine comes, constitute my main shoes, as well as a pair of funky cowboy suede fringe boots my friend gifted me. Layers are super important in the winter. Often, I have worn a vest top, long sleeve top, T-shirt on top then a jumper and jacket, alongside a pair of thermal tights under a pair of trousers and two pairs of socks. At my coldest, this was the maximum number of layers I wore. My wardrobe somehow is still as messy as it ever was when I had a bigger wardrobe but things move in and out much quicker than they used to.

Essential wardrobe items

- Vest tops
- Elasticated trousers aka hippy pants (according to my kids)
- T-shirts long sleeve and short sleeve
- Several dresses, formal and informal
- Underwear, although you may choose not to wear any, no judgement here
- A decent waterproof rain jacket and trousers
- Warm socks for winter and when you are in bed - I hate having cold feet in bed
- A cosy warm jumper and long cardigan
- Scarves for the winter to accessorise
- Several pairs of leggings
- Shorts

Kitchen Equipment

I don't know about you but I had cupboards full of Tupperware and more dishes and cutlery than I could eat from. I had steak knives, cheese knives and cutlery I wasn't even sure what it was for or had maybe used once.

I streamlined it down to four large plates, four small plates, several bowls, four sets of cutlery, one sharp knife for all chopping, a sieve and colander, saucepans of varying sizes, a large frying pan and a small one, a wooden spatula, a spoon with holes and a ladle. I brought chopsticks, which we have never used, and a deep pan to make popcorn which, six months later, is still waiting to be used. I picked up a slow cooker for free as a 'just in case my gas goes'. We don't have an oven in my caravan although some people do have microwaves or microwave ovens in their awnings. If we want pizza or fish and chips, we go out for it or grab a takeaway. Sainsburys also cook pizzas in-store much cheaper than take outs and they taste healthier. There are plenty of healthy meals you can make in a caravan. It's not all fry-ups. We have green soup once a week which is often made up of various leaves I have foraged or in-season veg. I also invested in a blender, not only for soups but also for smoothies and pestos for pasta. In summer, we eat a lot of salads, fresh fruit and vegetables. Winter is mostly stews, soups, curries and chillies. I have made a stickyweed pesto, dandelion leaf pesto and nettle pesto as well as nettle soup and dandelion leaf soup - all foraged not far from where I currently stay. I have also made my own herbal teas and the recipes can be found at the end of this book. I don't have a microwave or oven so everything is freshly made on a hob or under a grill.

Whilst living in my 3-bedroom rental, I had all the furniture I needed. I had a sofa bed, dining room table, chairs and beds. About six months before I moved, my kids had been jumping on my bed and broke the bed frame so that had already gone. After I bought my caravan in April 2021, I was asking in my mind, 'Am I meant to live in this or is it a weekend thing?' Within 24 hours, I had a message from a friend asking if I had any furniture he could have as he had just split up from his wife and was moving into a flat. I took photos of everything and sent them to him. He would take my table, a lamp, a mirror, a bookcase and the sofa bed. Another friend messaged the same day to ask if I knew of any houses to rent in the local area. 'OK, I'm listening', I said. Most of my furniture was second hand so I had no emotional ties to any of it and I didn't really want to pay extra for storing furniture that I didn't really love. There are numerous charity shops which will come and collect larger items for you if you can't sell them.

30/9/2020

Dear ones, we feel the anger rising

The anger rising in order to heal

The anger rising in order to change

To push ahead

To push through

Through the years that it's been suppressed

Through the years it's been pushed down

Your rage, your mothers' rage, your grandmothers' rage and beyond

Your rage, your fathers' rage, your grandfathers' rage and beyond

Be quiet, don't make a fuss, sshh, they said

Never allowed to voice our anger

Never allowed to voice our rage

Years of suppression

Being told what to do

Where to go, where to live

Who to be, what to buy?

Which car is the best?

Surely there is more

Remember you are unique, remember you are free

You have been conditioned

For centuries no less

No wonder the anger is rising

Transmute and release, transmute and release, transmute
and release

Let the anger go for the love to flow

Turn the rage to passion we cry

Where is it best used right now?

You can change and affect the world

All it takes is one, then two

Channel the anger and allow it to fuel

New creations, endeavours

New ways of working together

Collaborate and cooperate to build a new way

Release the anger and let love flow

Release the anger and let love flow

Release the anger and let love flow

Xx

Chapter 3- Choosing the Structure

It started, as always, with a thought. In March 2021, I started saying to my children, 'If mummy goes to live in a caravan, do you want to come and live with me?'

On 20 April, I woke up and saw a photo of a caravan on Facebook Marketplace. I pressed a button which automatically asked if it was available. 'Yes', came the reply. I wasn't doing anything that day so asked if I could pop over that morning to have a look at it. I knew nothing about caravans and literally had to rely on the chap selling it to show me what to do. I didn't have a towbar on my car or anywhere really to put it. I did check with my next-door neighbour if I could possibly put it on her driveway if I couldn't find anywhere. She said yes as long as she had somewhere to park her car. I got home and paid for the caravan. Thankfully, the chap said he was happy to have it on his driveway until I found a space for it. As I drove home, I rang my dad. 'Guess what, I've just bought a caravan!' My dad laughed. 'What you going to do, live in it?' 'I don't know yet.' As I continued driving, I kept laughing to myself, partly nervous and partly excited.

Part one of the offgrid adventure began or that is what it felt like. All I knew was that I needed somewhere with electricity and I was set.

Following this, I emailed twenty campsites in the York area to find one where my caravan could live and I found one, wahoo! I then had the issue of finding someone to tow it there. I asked on Facebook and a friend offered although he had a bad back. I rang the campsite on the off-chance and they had someone who could tow it for me that weekend. I met them at the campsite and watched as four guys very quickly unhooked it, put it into its space and jacked it up; then someone appeared with a spirit level, gave the nod that it was straight and it was done! One chap walked around my caravan and said, 'You'll need a water pump, a pipe for the waste, a battery (still haven't got that as I hooked up to the mains electric) and a low wattage kettle.' One of the most important things!

I quickly got to work, very enthusiastically, looking at ways to decorate my caravan as it looked dated with peach curtains and brown furniture. I painted the kitchen white, with one coat of primer and two coats of paint. I got halfway round and then lost said enthusiasm. I ripped the peach curtains out and, in the process, dislodged a piece of wood. The kids have managed to break one of the windows and one UV blind is broken so I have borrowed a piece of fabric from my neighbour to cover the window so the neighbours don't see me getting dressed. So, the caravan is half decorated and that's OK for now. I have to say though that my neighbour, Claire, laughed when I told her I had no gas or water hooked up to the caravan but I did have a statement wall! I painted around my mirror and one of the cupboard doors in a beautiful teal blue. Priorities, right?

Just to put things into perspective, the caravan I bought is a four berth, 17ft Coachman touring caravan and it cost £1800. It has a pull-out sofa that converts into like a king-size bed and two bunk beds. On the first night, I put the bunk beds up for the kids and instead they decided it would be more fun to sleep with me in a big bed. They never returned to the bunk beds. These are now used as a table and chairs for eating and crafting.

When I first bought the caravan, I have to admit that I didn't actually think I was going to live in it full-time. I kept asking 'upstairs' for signs. Shall I hand in my notice on my rental? Or should I keep it as an extra space? A couple of days later, I got a message from a friend who had split up from his wife and was moving into a new flat. 'Do you have any furniture I could have as I have no money?' I went round taking photos of my sofa bed, table, bookcases, mirrors, all my bulky furniture and said he could have everything. Another friend then got in touch to see if I was moving as they were looking for a rental. 'OK, OK, I'll hand my notice in!' This is how trusting I am with signs which are being sent. I handed in my notice and would be moving four weeks later.

What will you choose?

Many people are getting creative with their dwellings and some are amazing. It wasn't an option for me as I don't have all the practical skills for this. If you do however, this may be something to consider. People are using buses, ambulances and vans to be mobile and travel around the UK and Europe. You can buy mobile homes all ready to go and these are often around the £50k mark. Static caravans are a great transitional space as they are also fully equipped like a house. To buy, they can be around £30k plus or you can rent them from around £350 per month depending on where you go. It is always worth shopping around. Alternatively, you may want to buy a yurt if you have a space ready for it. I shared my thoughts on this in a YouTube video about what structures to live in. You can find the link to it at the end of the book. There are some restrictions on where you site your van/caravan but, the way I see it, the more of us choosing this way of life, the more we will gather and share information and knowledge from our individual experiences. There are lots of people on YouTube now sharing their skills and ideas. I have included some of these in the Resources section at the back of the book.

What to pack

I began transferring my particulars slowly and gradually, beginning with the kettle, sleeping bag and duvets, spare kitchen utensils, books I had been meaning to read but never got round to and clothes for the British summer. Note: always pack clothes for rain, sunshine, storms and hurricanes as you never know what a British summer will look like. Unfortunately, I obviously forgot what every other summer had been like and packed dresses, shorts and one hoody! Blankets and garden chairs were moved over with my candles and incense, a selection of kids' toys, board games, Top Trumps, a trampoline and our bikes. I took a selection of handy tools such as a saw, hammer, spanner and some pliers, my camping gear and wellies and a rag rug. I sold all of my furniture and put the remaining 'stuff' into storage. I managed to fit it into a 35 sq ft container which I have since downsized to 20 sq ft. It mostly consisted of boxes of kids' toys, an Ikea toy kitchen, a double mattress and some sentimental bits and bobs. If you are looking for affordable storage, this place was great and I got to drive a transit van for the first time!

https://www.gostore.co.uk/tell-a-friend/

In addition to what I brought, I also purchased the following which you can also buy:

- A warmer sleeping bag, after realising my first one wasn't worth the £10 I had paid for it - https://amzn.to/3hIElKy
- A low wattage kettle - https://amzn.to/3dQWmFn
- Paint
- Toilet cleaner - https://amzn.to/3AzGVLC
- Water pump - https://amzn.to/36jwaPv
- Awning. Mine is a Bradcot brand but you can easily get a second-hand one on eBay or Facebook Marketplace. Just check that the measurements are right and, if it doesn't come with an instruction manual, make sure you can get one online. Mine cost £300 but you can find them on eBay too.

12/6/2021

Five days until I move into the caravan. The kids' rooms have been emptied and everything apart from the kitchen is boxed up. Got a tip run to do tomorrow, two clients to see, kitchen to empty, garden, bikes, trampoline and then done. I think! I will miss the garden and the neighbours, the swallows flying overhead and the peace after a certain time of day. I saw a bird today that I have never seen in my garden before. It was a bullfinch. *A bullfinch is said to be an omen of exciting and joyful times on the horizon, encouraging you to relax and be open to the great times to be had. Associated with joy and happiness, Native Americans utilise the finch in celebratory ceremonies and festivals. A sense of freedom. Need to set a good example in your community and let people follow in your footsteps.*

Wow, how exciting is that. If you are already following me, you will know I am a huge fan of signs and synchronicities.

Do you ever just allow yourself to feel the heat of the sun on your closed eyelids?

To appreciate the warmth

Entering your divine vessel

You were born to do this

To jump

To lead

To not only have the vision but to then manifest it

Think it, feel it, allow it to happen

16/6/2021

Two more sleeps! Eek! All direct debits cancelled except mobile and internet. Nearly all packed, kids on airbeds in Alex's room tonight. Still no idea what to do about the trampoline or our bikes. I might have to leave them in the shed or the driveway until I find somewhere for them to go. Eve wants me to ask the campsite if we can take the trampoline there!

Taking stock of what the last three months have looked like I have:

- Completed my first seven-day master cleanse and lost 10lbs
- Worked
- Decluttered
- Bought a caravan
- Am moving semi offgrid
- Held my first plant medicine ceremony

What do I want from the next three months?

- More plant medicine ceremonies
- Discovering mugwort and working with her
- Fun, laughter, connection

- Adventure

Moving day

Moving day started at around 9am. I was on my period. However, you can't decide when your period comes so instead you have to get on with whatever you are doing on that day. My friend, Claire, offered to help then my other friend who had contacted me about the furniture also turned up with another friend. I went from having zero help to four of us. Wahoo! I had been with the kids to collect the transit van from the storage unit, had driven it halfway home then remembered my house keys were in the car back at the storage unit. Backwards and forwards we went and then started loading the van. I still hadn't dismantled the trampoline at this point. Thankfully, my friends helped out with that. Within about two hours, the van was loaded for the storage unit and bikes and trampoline were coming with us to the campsite.

I drove with my friend to the campsite and we offloaded the trampoline and bikes. I then headed off to the storage unit with the kids. It was a rainy day and I reversed into the bay ready to unload all of our stuff. Unfortunately, as I opened the side door, a range of items fell to the ground. Unloading this was going to take ages. As luck would have it, or the Universe was watching my back, there was a group of removal guys from Manchester who were on hand to help me. They loaded up trolleys with me and went up and down in the lift. One chap, who was Polish and used to fix caravans for a living, actually stacked my storage container in the best way possible. I was tired, exhausted and ready to cry and if it had been just me, I would literally have thrown stuff in every which way. Thankfully, he did it in an orderly fashion. I was so grateful to them and asked if I could give them some money for helping. 'No, no, no', they said. What about a hug? 'Ah yes', they said. So, hugs all round for these amazing guys whose names I didn't remember but whose kindness I always will.

Extras

I decided to buy an awning after seeing that everyone else on the site had one and they looked like a good idea. The word 'awning' wasn't even in my vocabulary until

2021. I had no idea how to put it up, no instruction manual, but a couple of the guys on site kindly offered to put it up for me in exchange for some beers. In the end, I paid with two bottles of squash and a Co-op Shepherd's Pie. I could get used to the idea of trading time for products. I was also kindly gifted some carpet for my awning from a friend who was selling her caravan; she just happened to have some offcuts from her hallway that she was going to put in the loft. It makes such a difference when you step outside in your bare feet onto soft cushioned carpet instead of pebbles. The next thing, which is a bigger purchase, is a tow bar for my car although I am not sure whether I can do that on my lease car or if I will have to change it. Anyway, for the minute, I am happy to have my caravan in one space and travel around camping. After a few weeks in the caravan, I realised that our caravan fridge wasn't big enough to hold enough food for the three of us so I purchased a second-hand one to put in my awning. Note that, during the winter, the freezer didn't work due to the cold conditions. However, it has been a godsend for keeping fruit and vegetables cool in the summer and plenty of ice pops in the freezer for the kids.

Anything else?

If you are planning to go offgrid, I highly recommend doing it bit by bit so that: a) it's not too much of a huge transition; and b) you have a chance to declutter massively before having to pay for storage. Personally, I would have kept a couple of boxes at my parents' house but my kids refused to let me get rid of their toys. Moving a vehicle to a campsite or a place with electric and running water may help with the transition or you may decide to fully jump into living in a field with nothing. Completely your choice and your journey. This is mine and, for now, this is where I am meant to be but who knows where I will end up!

As we adjusted to our new way of living, it felt initially like a long holiday. No freezer space, tiny fridge. Buying fresh fruit and veg from local greengrocers and farm shops then seeing some wilt in the blazing sweat box that the caravan becomes once it is over 25 degrees. It definitely felt like a new beginning yet also harks back to a time long ago. Within my memory somewhere, I know I have done this before. I have lived in a space not too dissimilar. Somewhere with land and space. A community. Learning to be with the land and seasons. Growing and harvesting. I know these memories will continue to come back. The knowing of the land, the trees, the birds. And I know I will remember and begin to identify the sights and sounds again. Even though some may cite this as a new beginning, in fact, I feel it's more of a coming home. And not just for me but for others too.

It has been nearly two months since I said goodbye to my home and moved into my caravan. It isn't fully renovated but it is halfway there. I am realising that there are things I brought which I really don't need such as way too many clothes. My wardrobe is half the size it was and there are still clothes in there that I haven't worn. I brought a load of toys and games for the kids which remain in the cupboards unplayed with. As long as we have books, paper, pens and outdoor toys we are sorted. My 10-year-old son learnt how to play badminton last week which resulted in me playing badminton for two and a half hours. The next day, my legs were aching. That is definitely one benefit of being here. I get to play with my children more. I get to spend actual time with them rather than tidying up or cleaning. I was never really a cleaner anyway but my point is that, when you have a house that is of a certain size, there is always something to be doing. My shopping lists are smaller as I have less space to store foods and when the sun shines the caravan turns into a mini sauna, so I need to choose foods that aren't perishable.

As the idea of moving offgrid becomes more appealing to people, I highly recommend following your heart and listening to your intuition on where you end up. For me, I know I am meant to be here at this time. I keep getting asked, 'What will you do at the end of October?' I don't know but for now I am happy where I am. Outside my window is a beautiful elder tree which is reminding me of the passing days. When I arrived, it was just beginning to flower and, as it flowered, I vowed to make elderflower cordial. Then, before I had a chance to do so, the flowers had gone and tiny green berries were beginning to appear. I will make elderberry syrup when the berries ripen. The pigeons cooing on the caravan roof, the sound of cows mooing in the distance. Occasionally, you hear a car driving by or a large tractor heading out to the fields. Then there is the sound of the campers - those who have come for a two-week break in the sun (sometimes, this is England!), wanting to make the most of being outdoors before returning to their homes. Some of them have been camping in this same space for many years and, for some, it's their first time.

The site itself is basic. It has what you need. Shower block and toilets. The Shack, as I call it, consists of three kitchen sinks, a huge washer and dryer and a variety of books and DVDs which you can borrow and return. I managed to find Miranda and Pitch Perfect 2 in amongst the numerous horror movies there. Not quite sure if that is telling of the people staying on the site but I am working to incorporate other titles in there. Likewise with the books. There are many romantic tales and books with little substance. In goes Matt Haig's 'The Midnight Library' and 'Healing is the New High' by Vex King. Pizza and burger menus adorn the notice board. There are some beautiful pots of rosemary as you drive in which I picked last week to make my smudge sticks with, to add some scent.

You feel as if you want to work with the land more whilst you are here. There are bird boxes in the trees that I can see from my window. Blue Tit and Robin chicks have been born in these trees and I often see the Blue Tits sat in the tree outside. I have started buying bird seed and fat balls to feed them. Herbs such as lavender, sage, basil and chives have been planted and I am picking them to dry for the winter months. I am wanting to drink teas made from our plants on the land. Recently, I was introduced to Mugwort by fellow Shaman and soul sister, Katharine. Unless you know what it is, you wouldn't see it but once you know what it is, you see it everywhere. I collected a few sticks and dried the leaves in my kids' wardrobe. It's the darkest and driest place in the caravan. I made a tea with some of the fresh leaves. Three leaves in a cup of hot water steeped for 10 minutes and drank it about half an hour before bed. I had some very vivid dreams over those few nights. Apparently, Mugwort can help with astral travelling as well as having medicinal benefits. The rest have been dried to add to teas at a later date and to smoke, as an experiment.

I feel so much more at peace here. Even whilst we have all the drama going on in the outside world and around Covid, it's as if that doesn't exist in my world. 'Ah well you're lucky', you might say. I choose not to watch or read the news as it lowers my vibration. If there is something that I really need to know, I am sure I will be given a head's up through my channelings or meditations or someone will tell me. My world right now is small. Smaller maybe than it has ever been. And that feels good. I am connecting with people in 'real' life, in the real world. Having conversations which are inspiring my soul and speaking into existence the life I want to co-create. There were no compost bins on site when I arrived and, at first, I was throwing away huge quantities of fresh food that had either quickly gone off or orange peels from juicing oranges. I found some free compost bins on Facebook and placed them in the campsite so people now have somewhere to throw their fresh fruit and veg peelings and garden waste. I can see myself building a yurt, although I don't quite know where yet! If you are looking for community and offgrid living, start small. Start with your neighbours and begin to watch it expand. For me, there is still some work to be done before we all arrive in our community spaces. It is gradual and will take some time. Inner work as well as the outer work must be done for us all to be able to co-exist in these communities. It is no good building lots of homes and huts if we then don't know how to communicate about something which may have irked us. Within all communities, there will be a variety of roles to help support not just in the architecture and building structure but also with the emotional and healing side. Peacekeepers and action takers. Yes, we can all do these different roles but sometimes one may be in a better place than another to take it on for the day. Many hats we will wear. Gardener, teacher, student, builder, friend, etc. Whatever you are most passionate about, stand up for and enjoy it. You can then share your passion amongst the community.

We are returning to an old way of living and the question of money often arises. How am I going to afford that? We can't afford to buy land, what shall we do? What is meant for you will not pass you by. I can't remember who said that or I would quote them but it is true.

There are a variety of people on the site, all with their own stories. What I love though is the feeling of community that is already here. As you get to know people, there are offerings of help. As you leave the site, asking if anyone needs anything from the shop. Small things like that matter. To me anyway. Knowing that there are people around you that you can ask for help. I bought some awning for my caravan. I didn't even know what awning was until I got the caravan and wondered what the extra fabric bits were on everyone's caravans. I bought one second-hand from a lady in Castleford. It lay in my caravan for three weeks as I deliberated how to put it up. There were no instructions in the bag. Thankfully, several of the guys on site had already put a few up so were happy to help with mine. I watched and tried to help but ended up having to leave after a couple of hours as the kids were getting bored. When I returned, my awning was up and I was ready to fill it. But with what? There were grass roots coming through the stones. I had offered to visit a friend's caravan and check it out for another friend. As I was leaving my friend's house, she just happened to say, 'You don't need any carpet, do you?' 'Erm, yes that would be perfect for my awning thank you'. Got home and placed the carpet on my awning floor. The only problem was that it is cream and, with two kids, it wouldn't be staying that colour for long. A local furniture/secondhand shop had a room full of bits and bobs for £1. I found three throws, a large red one and two lilac-coloured. They would do to throw over the carpets for now. One of the first things I created in my awning was a small altar area. This consists of my candles, crystals, Oracle cards and feathers. I have been collecting feathers from the campsite and planning on making a feather headdress with them. It has provided extra space that has been used for yoga, dancing, reading and, most recently, a badminton court. I have to say, I am very grateful for this extra living space area.

I have decided for now not to attach my water barrel. The sink space actually serves as an extra storage unit for now for fruit and jars and the shower space holds my washing basket. I walk to the Shack daily to wash my pots and pans and dishes. The Shack also houses a huge washing machine and dryer so I can wash my clothes once a week instead of three times a week which I was doing previously. I just realised yesterday that the mirrors I thought were ridiculously placed on the sides of the walls next to the sink, like who can look at their face from that angle, actually have small hinges underneath which allow the mirrors to move so you can see your face without twisting it sideways.

There is, I feel, some caravan etiquette which may be unspoken so, until you cross the line, you have no idea what it is. These are some of the things I have picked up so far

- When calling on neighbours, knock on their caravan wall. If they want to see you or speak to you, they will respond. If not, they won't. Or they could be out. Or maybe that's just when I knock?

- If they have an awning, always take your shoes off when you first go in even if, like mine, the floor is often covered in grass, sticks, soil and plant bits from myself and the kids.

- When you are popping out to the shops, always ask people if there is anything they need. It's just plain courtesy and there may be a day where you need something and can't get to the shop.

- No one ever seems to ask why you are here or what you are doing here and you don't ask them unless they are willing to volunteer their story. As one caravanner said, 'We all have a story'.

- If you are cooking something and have extras, offer them out. Unfortunately, the idea of a lentil dahl curry didn't go down so well with some of the guys but the offer was there and was politely refused.

- Let people know what you are good at and find out what they are good at too. You can then swap skills and save you both some money.

Chapter 4 - Finding your Tribe

When I started this journey, I didn't know anyone who was living offgrid or even wanted to. I started talking to people about it and soon found that there were other people like me.

One week, I met up with three ladies who all had a similar vision. We all wanted to create our own offgrid communities complete with a healing centre. What are the chances?

I ran a Lionsgate Portal meditation in August 2021 and every single lady wanted to be part of a community. I decided to set up a group around York called Conscious Community Gathering and invite anyone who was interested in going offgrid along. I think there were twenty-five of us in total, a mixture of ages, some with families and some without. This was before lockdown. Some of us have stayed in touch and some of us are still working towards it. If you can't find a group that meets your needs, go out and create your own group.

There are so many groups now with a similar vision

which is great to see. We have the Offgrid Community Network UK on Telegram which I am a facilitator of and I created Awakened Offgrid Communities UK over on Facebook. There is The Community on Telegram, JoinaVision, Stand Up in the Parks across the UK and a whole host of other groups which may be of benefit to you. Rather than standing on the sidelines, jump in. Where can you be of service within the group? What skills can you share? What questions do you have? Get to know people on an individual level too.

One of our facilitators, Lawrence, always says to people, 'Go out and volunteer'. Find something you can get into nearby. It may not be a fully-fledged community set-up but it might be a community garden. This is where Kate Brown, founder of the network, started and now she is helping build a community in Scotland. Join local groups, visit local communities or offer ones. There is so much work going on right now to build these amazing spaces for not only ourselves but others too.

It is also worth thinking about what sort of community you want to live in. Many of us have these dreams that we will enter into a community and everything will be beautiful and easy. If that's you, please know that it isn't always easy and there will be 'stuff' that comes up to work through, whether by yourself or with others. How do we communicate with others? How are we going to resolve conflicts when living in such close proximity to others? What happens if you move into a community and then decide you don't want to be there. These aren't just questions for you; as I'm typing them it is also helping me work through what I envisage for a community. My personal feeling is that it is to do with values. Are your values aligned with the community's?

I visited my first community house share during 2020 in Glastonbury. I remember sitting there asking 'upstairs' as I call it why I needed to be there. 'It's not about you, Glastonbury needed your energy'. It felt like a telling off. It was amazing to see how it worked but I knew I had to come back to York and find my own space to build a community.

Some communities are based on religious beliefs such as the Buddhist Centre in Pocklington; others may be based on spiritual beliefs such as Findhorn, Scotland. It is up to you to research and find the right space for you.

Chapter 5 - Money and Finances

The biggest advantage of staying in a caravan is the amount of money you are going to save on your bills; your rent/mortgage, water, Council Tax, electric, gas and broadband. Costs are minimised which, again, allows you some freedom to do a bit more of what you want to do instead of what you have to do.

You may find yourself, as I have done, spending more money currently, on fuel and food. They are the two biggest expenses I currently have. My Calor Gas bottle, which I got in April 2021, lasted until October and cost me £60 to refill. We are currently at the end of January and I still haven't had to fill it up. My electric is currently plugged into the mains but I could get a 12V battery. If you are on Universal credit, you can still claim for site fees.

Prior to moving, I began to cancel or stop paying certain bills. I stopped paying my water bill as a friend of mine had shared that she hadn't paid in seven years and had never been cut off. I then stopped paying my Council

Tax. I wanted to experiment and see for myself what worked and what didn't. Yorkshire Water kept calling so I stopped answering my phone. My credit card company chased me incessantly for several months. When I tried to call one back to tell them that they were harassing me, no one answered the phone. It is up to you whether you want to take risks such as these or not. I am merely sharing my experience. There are more legitimate ways you can do this by writing to them, sending their letters back, using common law, etc, but for me I didn't want to put my energy into that. My energy was to focus on leaving the old way of living and heading to a new one.

Can I still work in a caravan?

Of course. There are lots of Sim card packages out there now which offer unlimited data, texts and calls for £20 per month. I am currently with Smarty. My son, who is 10 years old, taught me how to use my mobile phone as a router and tether my laptop to the internet. So frigging clever! If you are working online but worried about not being able to, unless you are truly going offgrid with no electric and living in the middle of a mountain range, the chances of you being able to continue to work are quite high. And, of course, there are many other ways to earn a living and work, whether you choose to run workshops in a particular subject you are knowledgeable about, teach or do odd jobs if you are skilled. If you want to look after children, you can do that. Write a book. The various ways to earn a living are endless and there are many opportunities around. My suggestion would be to do what feels most aligned with you. What do you enjoy doing? What feels right? It is so much more fun to do this than being told to sit in an office typing names and numbers all day every day. I worked in data entry for the Inland Revenue for six months whilst saving to go to Mexico when I was nineteen. Anyway, I digress. Do what you love and if you don't know what you love then spend some time finding out what interests you. Gardening, herbs, plants, healing, writing, drawing, crafting, making candles. Follow your heart. I have created a PDF of all the ways I can think that you can earn money offgrid which you can grab here. (Link also in Resources)

21/11/2021

Walking through the local woods, I found myself on a path not well trodden. As I stumbled along and found myself walking sideways, holding onto trees, I cursed out loud. I cried. I could see the well-established path below me. Why hadn't I chosen that path? Why was I not following the path that everyone else was on? Why do I have to walk the path less trodden? I cried into the abyss. I felt angry and annoyed. It would be so much easier. 'Yes', I heard a voice say, 'but that is not your path. You came to forge new ones. At times, it may feel difficult and lonely but you are showing others the way forward'.

Sometimes, I don't like the messages I am given and this was one of those times. Thankfully, there was no one else around to witness my stumbling, haphazard way of walking through the woods. I knew when I left that I had received some important insight which in time would propel me forward.

Winter in a caravan

28/11/2021

The coldest day so far in the caravan. -1 degrees, woke

up and felt strangely blessed. The sunset was beautiful and I felt in a good mood. My gas pipes froze and I couldn't make the porridge I so meticulously prepared with oats, apple, raisins, cinnamon and nutmeg. Fuck! Thankfully, due to a previous camping trip, I had a gas stove in my outdoor storage box. Forty-five minutes later, my porridge was ready and I was uber grateful for it. My caravan was cold so I borrowed an electric radiator from a friend who had said I could borrow it if I ever felt cold. To say I was toasty would be an understatement. When we are in a house and have gas and electric on tap, these things can be taken for granted. When you are in a place where water, gas and electric aren't always available, you may find yourself feeling vulnerable. At the site I am on is a shack where I wash and dry my clothes and dishes. This week, I put my clothes in the washing machine only for them to come out wet. I put another £3 in and the same thing happened. The tumble dryer couldn't dry them properly. I hung them in my awning and tried gradually drying them. Unfortunately, half of my washing just smelled of damp. Then a notice appeared, 'Washing machine out of order'. I had used a launderette previously but, at £16 a binbag, it wasn't cheap. I was meant to be meeting up with a lady and her 13-year-old. The day before we were due to meet, she said, 'If you need any washing doing, bring it over'. Ah my days, yes! Such gratitude! When we have decided to live in a space that isn't conventional shall we say, an invitation for washing, a bath, lunch or dinner is probably one of the best things that another human can offer us.

02/12/2021

Yesterday, we put our Xmas tree up. When I say Xmas tree, it was a chopped down fir tree from the site we are staying on. We tried putting it in a bucket full of soil but it kept falling over so I invested in a tree stand from The Range. Even though I am gradually working my way out of the commercial aspect of Xmas, there is something that I love about going to the Range and seeing their Xmas decorations and lights. In 2020, I walked around and cried thinking it may be the last year I would see them. However, they were still around and I needed a Xmas tree stand. Since I got divorced, one of our family traditions has been to buy a decoration for the tree every year. Adorning our fir tree in our awning is a pink glittery unicorn, a glistening white star and a more natural style dream catcher, a set of lights my daughter won last week at a school Xmas fayre and a set of snowflake lights I bought from Sainsburys. It's not 100% natural, it's not colour coordinated but it's ours.

Today, we went for a walk in the woods to collect some greenery to make a wreath. My expertise does not lie in crafting but I am always willing to give things a go. I found a wire coat hanger and we wrapped around ferns, firs and holly. It was messy but again we hung it in our awning. I have decided this year not to buy into the advent calendar thing. Next year, I may actually plan for it but for this year I'm not. The kids have one at their dad's.

The worst thing for me is changing the toilet. The smell hits you as you empty it. Personally, I would rather have a compost toilet so it just went in and you would never have to deal with it again. However, where I am means that I have to deal with my shit, literally. It stinks and I hate it but needs must.

I feel I am halfway to my offgrid dream but not there yet. I know I will get there but as yet I am not sure when. My journey has been amazing, ups and downs, highs and lows. Would I recommend this to anyone else? Hell yeah! You don't realise until you have done this how resilient you are, how adaptable and courageous. You are so much stronger than you know and whether for you offgrid living involves three months initially, or six months, a year or an eternity - this is your journey. We are all pioneers and learning to listen to our heart and soul can truly help us in learning to let go of all we know and embrace all we do not know.

Chapter 6 - Creating a Strong Foundation for yourself

Creating a strong foundation, for me, was essential. I trusted every day that I was making the right decision and I had faith that I would go wherever I was meant to. This was due to the work I had done previously on myself over a number of years. (You can find out more about this in my first book, 'A Gentle Hug for the Soul'). I am fairly resilient and happy to go with the flow, most of the time. It takes courage to step out of the system you were born into an embrace a new way of living. There is definitely a period of transition needed as you begin to adapt to a slower pace of life. Some days, you will just want to lie on your sun lounger and read your book. Some days, you might draw. Time seems to blur as there are no clocks to look at, except on your phone. Mornings are slower and it can be lunchtime before you are ready to go anywhere. You have less 'stuff', less to clean, less to wash, less to be busy with which then frees up time to get creative, to read, to actually enjoy doing things you want to do instead of having to do.

When you begin to leave the structures that have been built for us, it can bring up a lot of fear. Fear of the unknown is a huge one. Way back in 2011, I was on honeymoon in the Maldives. It was such a beautiful space but all I could think about was the terrible weather back in the UK. It was snowing and I had already skidded on the ice, crashing my car once. I was lying on a massage bed, face down, watching the fishes when I heard this booming voice saying, 'Fear not the unknown'. Since then, this has become a mantra of mine for whenever I have felt fear arise within me.

The practical side for me is the easier bit. Working on your emotional side and personal development whilst moving is also something I strongly recommend. You might want to get started straight away and throw yourself into a new project. Are you mentally ready? Do you feel you have the tools to equip yourself emotionally? If not, I suggest beginning some sort of practice which is going to help you. There will be days you feel angry, sad, happy, frustrated. How do you currently manage these emotions? Living in a smaller space, you may feel as if you need to be outside more. Walking outside and being in nature is a huge benefit to offgrid/outdoor living.

My toolbox looks a bit like this and it may not be for everybody but it has seriously helped me over the last twelve months.

- Meditation
- Yoga
- Reading
- Journaling
- Healing in whatever form feels right for you
- Working with plant medicine
- Walks in nature
- Meeting up with friends and chatting to supportive people
- Being in groups with likeminded souls, whether on Facebook or Telegram, with people who are already doing what I am looking to do. (You can find links at the end of the book for resources currently available).

Whatever your self-care plan looks like for you, ensuring that you have a routine or a practice which will support you through any emotions which may come up during this time is extremely helpful. When we are in a calm and peaceful space, we make better decisions; when we come from our hearts, we make better decisions. When we come from a space of anger, fear and rage, we make rash decisions which can often leave us feeling annoyed or frustrated. It takes time to settle into your new space, your new way of living for yourself and your family. Be patient, kind and compassionate and then go for a scream in the woods if it is all getting too much. Honour your boundaries and those of others.

It takes courage to make a leap into the unknown. Legally, you can live in a touring caravan all year round. However, you will need an address for your banking, post, etc. This is where friends and family can help. You will also need to find a site which allows you to stay there for twelve months of the year, if that is what you want. If you want to travel around in your caravan and explore then, obviously, you can do but I would recommend doing some research to find spaces for the winter months. Not all sites will allow you to stay all of the time. You can purchase a piece of land and put your caravan on it. The main reason, I see, as to why the UK government doesn't want you to live in this way, is because you won't be paying Council Tax on your caravan.

You need to be focused on your reasons for doing this and not allow anyone to talk you out of it. I wrote earlier of some of the challenges you may face - well, this is one of them. I have been extremely lucky that my friends and family have been supportive in how I am choosing to live. However, there are people who have tried to exert their opinions on me and tell me I am better off living in a house. They don't pay my bills. If I was living in a house, by myself, I would have little disposable income and would be under huge financial pressure as a single mum. I know this would also affect my mental health and emotional wellbeing. We have to balance everything up and choose what is right for us. Mindset is key when we choose a different path for ourselves and our family. I'm not the first person to do this and certainly won't be the last. One chap I have come across on my journey has been living in a caravan in a forest for the last twenty-five years and loves it. Hearing from people like this inspires me to keep going. Learning to spend time by myself is something I have become accustomed to over the last four years since my divorce and, to be honest, I truly appreciate the time I have to myself. I am happy in my own company. I make myself laugh, and cry, sometimes. I know when I am feeling like I need space and when I want to be sociable. I would never describe myself as an introvert and those who know me wouldn't either. I love being around other people and thrive on it but I also love spending time alone. When we are in full-time jobs, working and living in a house, we get used to being busy. When the busyness drops away and there is only you, what does your life look like? Do you have hobbies? What do you love to do? If you can't answer right now, that's OK. I've been there myself and it has taken me time to adjust and learn what I love about me and my life whilst here. I love writing and drawing and I have recently started watercolour painting. I love to dance in my caravan to old 90s dance tunes and sing at the top of my voice. I love walking in nature and noticing the beauty in the great outdoors. Learning to become comfortable doing nothing can take time in itself so be patient with yourself.

Loneliness vs solitude

I often feel a need for solitude. To have time alone with my thoughts. Time for me. For my imagination to wander. Time for me. To have a bath. Time for me. To meditate. Loneliness is different. Loneliness comes in when we have a want to be with other people. A want to be sociable. A want to connect. It is part of our human nature that we socialise. Solitude is choosing to spend time alone. Loneliness is feeling alone. When you have a faith or belief in the Universe or God or Source, you never feel alone. You have a knowing that you are protected; that there are angels, spirits, guides around you keeping you safe. Solitude is a choice, loneliness isn't.

Are we born resilient or is it learned? I remember asking someone this a few years ago and, to be honest, I still don't have the answer. What I do know is that the more I have pushed myself out of my comfort zone or gone through a difficult period in my life, I have grown from it. Maybe this is where resilience comes from. Being willing to give something new a 'go' and willing to explore other ways of being. When we put ourselves into new environments or new places, we feel vulnerable as it is new and something we haven't done before. We have to get comfortable with feeling uncomfortable. Asking others who have more experience for help may be something we aren't accustomed to. Society tells us we must rely on ourselves, be independent and, to an extent, this is true. I am reminded of the Destiny's Child song, 'Independent Women'. Yes, there are times when we need to be independent but, with the offgrid journey, there are also times where we need to be able and willing to ask for help. We don't have all the skills ourselves to build a community. Together, we can learn and use our strengths to build communities going forward. If you do have all the skills, amazing! If you don't, work with your strengths but be willing to learn more.

Chapter 7 – Food and Foraging

Food

My caravan has an integral fridge, the problem being that it isn't much larger than two shoeboxes. I can fit my milk in the doorway, some spreadable butter, jam and some jars. My freezer can fit a pack of sausages. With two children, I needed a larger fridge so I got one from a local second-hand store for £40 and plugged it into my awning. It also has a bigger freezer which was ideal for ice pops for over the summer. The downside was that, during the cooler weather, when you most want a freezer, it stopped working as it was too cold in the awning. I don't tend to do big shops anymore, instead shopping more regularly and buying fresh fruit and veg.

As the darker months set in, I realised that the mice were coming into my awning so I got a plastic box to put my onions and garlic, the kids crisps and baked goods in. I used my kitchen sink to store my fruit. I make sure I keep cans of chopped tomatoes and coconut milk in my cupboard as well as store essentials such as lentils, pasta, rice and eggs. I have also been working with the herbs and berries growing around me to make my own teas and recently made a delicious rosemary pesto for pasta or potatoes. The recipe is at the back of the book.

Please bear in mind that I am not a qualified herbalist. I am merely sharing my knowledge and experience that I have gained over the last twelve months. As I have been drawn to working with and foraging local herbs and plants, I have found there are some Apothecary staples which everyone must have in their cabinet. You may find other essentials and I hope you do but, if you are just getting started, these can be a good guide.

Apothecary Staples

- Olive oil
- Sea salt
- Honey
- Apple cider vinegar
- Baking soda
- Beeswax
- Sweet Almond oil
- Coconut oil

Equipment

- Weighing scales
- Measuring jug
- Saucepans
- Mixing bowls
- Sieve
- Blender
- Whisk
- Pestle and Mortar

With your own apothecary, you can begin to make so many items and products, not only for yourselves but also for your friends and family.

Grapefruit and Peppermint Body scrub

½ cup coconut oil

¼ cup demerara sugar

Grapefruit zest (you can choose how fruity you want to make it)

8 drops peppermint oil

Melt your oil, stir in the sugar, zest and peppermint oil. Pour into a container of your choice and, ta dah, you have your own body scrub.

<u>Toothpaste</u>

6 tablespoons of coconut oil

4 tablespoons of baking soda

20 drops of oil of oregano

20 drops of peppermint oil

Blend all together and put in a jar. This will last around three to five months.

Herbs Foraged and Used in Teas and Tinctures

Mugwort (Forage between July and September in UK)

Artemesia vulgari

Not a traditional herbal tea or as well-known as many others, Mugwort has become more fashionable in 2021. I had never heard of it until it happened to be mentioned several times in a conversation and then kept popping up everywhere, as things do. I was looking for it but couldn't see it until a friend showed me exactly where to find it and what it looked like. I picked a handful of branches and began to work with her. Mugwort feels like a more feminine plant which has nurturing qualities and works with women, not only in their physical cycles but also to help open us up to other worlds.

Considered the universal herb for protection and prophecy – also used for pain, healing, psychic powers and lucid dreaming. Known as a common weed, this plant grows across the UK and can reach heights of up to six feet tall, with beautiful silvery shimmering leaves and stalks which can be used as part of magical fire ceremonies. It is mostly found along the roadside and the Romans used to stop on their marches to drink it and as a rub for their feet.

Mugwort, or hogwart as a friend of mine calls it, has magical powers which would certainly fit in with a Harry Potter movie. Drinking Mugwort tea can help with lucid dreaming and astral travelling. My dreams are certainly more vivid on the evenings I drink this tea. Mixing it with honey or maple syrup will sweeten it as it does have a slightly bitter taste. A friend of mine adds milk to hers.

Working with Mugwort has been an exciting journey,

not only for myself but also for my clients. One client's husband accidentally added it to their pasta sauce and declared he felt a bit spacey afterwards.

Benefits

- Menopause relief
- Joint pain relief
- Can help to alleviate digestive and intestinal issues
- Can aid astral travelling and lucid dreaming
- Supports women with their menstrual cycles

Uses

Once mugwort has dried (I hung mine up in my awning), you can use the leaves to make tea or to smoke. The tea can be drunk in the evening before bed and is said to help with lucid dreaming and astral travelling. I used the sticks to burn in ceremony and also made some mugwort smudge sticks. I prepare a tincture using vodka and mugwort which I now sell on my Etsy store. You will also find the link in Resources.

Who is it not for?

Do not use if pregnant or breastfeeding

Hawthorn (Foraged in September)

Crataegus laevigata

A beautiful red, vibrant berry which makes its appearance around September time. The leaves are beautiful dried and stewed in a tea. Finding these beautiful little berries along a path one day, I knew I needed to connect with this fruit to see how we can work with it. Having made tinctures and teas, the benefits of this beautiful berry are huge, especially for those with cardio or heart problems. The berries were a favourite of the Native Americans as a heart tonic and also used for gastrointestinal complaints. Prescribed by Ancient Greek physician Dioscorides in the 1st century AD as a remedy for heart problems.

Benefits

Hawthorn berries contain powerful antioxidants. They can help to keep blood pressure in check. They can also increase blood flow to the heart by dilating the peripheral and coronary blood vessels. High in oligomeric procyanidins (OPCs). Can improve circulation, strengthen capillaries, reduce inflammation, boost the immune system, are effective antioxidants for the brain and nerve tissue and enhance connective tissue health. Stimulates bile and gastric secretions, aiding in the digestion of stagnant food in the GI tract.

Uses

The berries can be dried or used fresh. They can also be used in teas, tinctures and powders. The leaves can be dried for tea or you can also use the berries. Tinctures can be made up for those suffering with heart problems. Again, I have worked with it and made my own tinctures.

Who is it not for?

Can interact with prescription medication including beta blockers and calcium channel blockers and medications that increase blood flow to the heart.

Rosehips (Foraged between September and December)

Rosa Canina

Rosehips are a beautiful flower which adorn our hedgerows from September through to December. Often found next to a hawthorn tree, they are often oval shaped with small green shoots from one end. When I was younger, I remember kids from school would often pick these, open them up and stick them down other kids' jumpers as the seeds and hairs inside can be itchy. They were known as 'itch bombs' back then. I never fully knew the benefits of these amazing fruits until I decided to investigate them further. I, myself, have been experimenting, making tinctures, oils and teas and would love to hear whether you pick them and, if so, what you make with them.

Rosehips contain sixty times more Vitamin C than one orange! They also contain antioxidants and flavonoids which are anti-inflammatory. As an external oil, it can help stimulate collagen and benefits your skin with skin brightening properties. It can help create a more youthful, radiant, glowing complexion. It is known as a dry oil and so it soaks easily into the skin.

Benefits

Rosehips can also be used internally through tinctures or capsules or tea. The benefits of rosehips are:

- Can help combat adrenal fatigue
- Can help relieve pain felt from arthritis
- Can help prevent diabetes

- Can help lower cholesterol

There are many other benefits from this beautiful fruit which are still being researched.

<u>Uses</u>

You can drink them as a tea, make a tincture, dry them and powder them or make an oil with them for your skin.

Rosehip facial oil is a beautiful luxurious oil for the skin. High in vitamin C content, it helps stimulate collagen and benefits your skin with skin brightening properties. It allows your skin to look more youthful, radiant and glowing. The colour is like a rich amber gold. It absorbs quickly into the skin and leaves a smooth residue on the surface. It smoothes fine lines and wrinkles. Suitable for vegans and 100% natural. What more could you want for your skin?

You can grab a bottle of Temple Woman Rosehip Facial Oil here. The link can also be found in Resources.

Nettles
Urtica dioica

Ah, the humble nettle, known as a weed in most of the UK. I remember sitting on a stinging nettle plant once as a young girl and wow the pain! Unlike anything I had felt before. I have steered clear of them for many a year since. However, this year, I have been surrounded by nettles so I decided to do a bit of research into them and found some amazing benefits of working with these plants.

Firstly, did you know there is a male and female stinging nettle? And that it is the seed of the female nettle that is most powerful in herbal remedies? Awesome stuff! Apart from stinging myself a couple of times whilst drying and removing the seeds from the nettle plants, it was definitely not as painful as sitting in them as a young girl!

Benefits

There are so many benefits from nettles but here are just a few!

- Contains Vitamin A which is good for eye health
- Nettle leaf can help with arthritis when wrapped around the joint
- Can help increase your energy levels
- Can help treat eczema

- Helps strengthen bones and connective tissue
- Promotes urinary system health by acting as a diuretic
- Is a great hair tonic

<u>Uses</u>

In the springtime, you can pick them in the early morning and use in soups or teas. You can dry the nettle leaves in a dark place to use later in the year. Collecting the nettle seeds took some time and one evening I sat with my neighbour, Pauline, using a fork to take the seeds from the plant. The seeds can be dried and used in smoothies.

Willow Bark

Salix Alba

As I was researching other ingredients that I could add to my own apothecary, I felt strongly drawn to willow bark. I had looked it up on an ingredient website but really wanted to collect by own willow bark. I couldn't think where I could find a willow tree locally so I thought I would wait until it appeared. And appear it did. One evening, whilst picking up a friend from Stamford Bridge, a man walked behind my car and announced very loudly to his family, 'Look at that beautiful willow tree'. My ears pricked up. Yay, finally. I waited for the family to pass before getting out of the car and walking in the dark to the willow tree. I couldn't quite see where the grass ended and the river began so I asked the tree if I could take a branch and popped it into the boot of my car. The next day, I picked all of the leaves off to dry and whittled the branches to dry the bark to make a tea, which I have to say wasn't too unpleasant, except when I forgot to take the bark out the first time and was literally drinking bark. If making a tea, I suggest steeping it and removing the bark before drinking.

Used by Ancient Egyptians as far back as 3000 BC to treat several ailments. Native Americans used it to reduce fever. Hippocrates recommended using extracts of willow bark to alleviate the pain of childbirth and reduce fever. White willow trees (salix alba) grow a bark that contains the chemical called salicin which has anti-inflammatory effects. Salicin works in similar ways as acetylsalicylic acid, the active ingredient in aspirin. In fact, in the 1800s, Salicin was used to develop aspirin.

<u>Benefits</u>

Again, there are a number of benefits of the willow tree. Here are just a few:

- Used for pain including headaches, muscle or joint pain
- Can help with pain from rheumatoid arthritis, osteoarthritis and gout
- Anti-inflammatory, antipyretic (fever reducing) analgesic
- Can ease chronic lower back pain
- Helps ease menstrual cramps

<u>Uses</u>

If you find your own willow tree, you can make a tea, tincture, oil or powder with the bark. The best time to harvest the bark is in the springtime. However, please don't go carving up the trees if you aren't sure what you are doing as it can also cause the tree a lot of damage.

<u>Common side effects</u>

Increase in blood pressure, gastrointestinal problems. Children under sixteen and pregnant or breastfeeding women should not be given this tea.

As with all herbal medicines and supplements, do check with your GP before taking as some may interact with current medication. If you are foraging to make your own tinctures and remedies, remember to be mindful of leaving some berries for the birds and the other insects who may also be relying on them.

Oregano (Forage throughout the year if self-grown)

Origanum vulgare

Oregano is a well-known herb use mostly in pizza and pasta sauces. Often adorning a garden herb box, many of us may just use it for culinary purposes. I myself, have had a window box full of oregano since the summer and, it was only whilst passing it today, I wondered what else I could use it for. How can this herb be of benefit to us?

Firstly, one teaspoon of oregano fulfils 8% of our daily vitamin K needs. It is high in antioxidants and is antibacterial and antiviral. Oregano has forty-two times the antioxidant level of apples and four times that of blueberries.

Benefits

- Can aid in digestion
- Can improve heart and bone health
- High in vitamins A, C and E
- Can boost your immunity during cold and flu season
- Can fight against aging and may reduce body fat

Uses

I have dried the leaves and ground them up for food as well as creating oregano oil using olive oil and oregano. This can be used for a variety of things. I use it in my toothpaste that I made for myself and sometimes use it as a mouthwash.

Rosemary

Rosmarinus Officinalis

I have always loved the smell of rosemary and, whilst walking past several plant pots full of it, I thought I would collect some and see what else I could do with this fragrant herb. Its medicinal use can be dated back to the Greeks and Romans. It is a herb that is associated with remembrance. Greek students used to wear hair garlands made of rosemary.

Benefits

- Antioxidant and anti-inflammatory
- A cognitive stimulant
- Can help boost the immune system and improve blood circulation
- Helps improve memory performance
- Boosts alertness, intelligence and focus
- Oil of rosemary promotes hair growth, prevents baldness and can slow greying
- Use for digestive problems

Uses

There are so many amazing things you can do with rosemary. I dried some in my kids' wardrobes but the bits went everywhere. Another batch, I left in a Morrison's paper bag for several weeks and it was perfect. You can make a tea and use in cooking. I made a delicious vegan pesto and have popped the recipe below. I also made a rosemary oil for hair growth. Years ago, I was at a well-known hairdresser in Manchester. I remember them saying that I had a receding patch on the side of my head. It isn't obvious to anyone else but I have started massaging the oil into the space to encourage my hair to grow.

<u>Rosemary Pesto</u>

Bear in mind that rosemary has quite a strong taste. The pesto is ideal for pasta or potatoes.

Handful of rosemary

2 garlic cloves

Pine nuts

Salt & pepper

Olive oil

Vegan nutritional flakes

Blend together or use a pestle and mortar to crush it altogether. If too dry, add a bit more olive oil; if too wet, add some more flakes.

Stir into your pasta or your potatoes.

<u>Rosemary Tea</u>

Soak a handful of the herbs in a teapot.

Mullein

Verbascum Thapsus

As with most of the herbs I have included here, it wasn't until I was in London with the kids and developed a horrendous cough that I discovered mullein. Thankfully, we were only fifteen minutes away from one of the oldest apothecaries in London so we hot footed it down there to grab a tincture. Unbeknownst to me, this amazing plant had been growing in the front garden of the house I used to live in. Every year, I would think how pretty it looked and then pull it out once the flowers had died back. It has beautiful sage-like leaves, but larger with a silvery fur and a stalk rising to a top with yellow flowers.

Benefits

Mullein has various benefits but primarily can be used to help treat coughs, colds and asthma. Used to treat respiratory conditions, reduces inflammation, effective against flu and is antiviral and antibacterial. It was introduced to the Native Americans by early settlers. The Navajo were known to smoke the leaves to treat asthma and clear lung congestion. They are rich in saponins and the most popular remedies are for earache and ear infection.

Uses

Although I never got the chance to pick this beautiful

plant whilst in season, it is one that I will be keeping an eye out for this year.

Stickyweed

Galium Aparine

Also known as cleavers, goosegrass or sticky willie. You may remember this as the weed that you would pick on the way to school and throw on people's clothes so it would stick to them. But did you know it has so many amazing benefits? I wrote a blog on the five surprising benefits of stickyweed on my website http://www.lindsaybanks.uk/blog It is extremely abundant around April/May time.

It is derived from the Greek word for 'milk' because the flowers were used to curdle milk in cheese making. Aparine is a name used by Theophrastus. It means 'clinging' or 'seizing' and is derived from the Greek απαίρω apairo 'lay hold of, seize', itself coming from από 'from' + αίρω 'pull to lift'. Wikipedia.

Benefits

- Used to boost the immune system
- Supports and cleanses the lymph system

- Can help reduce swollen glands

- Supports the kidneys and acts as a diuretic

- Helps reduce fine lines and wrinkles when used as a face wash

<u>Uses</u>

This plant/weed is edible. The leaves and stems of the plant can be cooked as a leaf vegetable if gathered before the fruits appear. The fruits have often been dried and roasted and then used as a coffee substitute which contains less caffeine.

<u>Stickyweed Pesto recipe</u>

Handful of stickyweed

Handful of spinach or other greens such as dandelion leaves or wild garlic

1 garlic clove

Coconut oil

Salt and pepper

Nutritional flakes

Use pestle and mortar to crush or throw it all in a blender. Once blended or crushed, stir into cooked pasta. Note that I used raw stickyweed; some recipes advise that you blanch it before making into a pesto. I was left with a clump of greenness at the end of blending which may not have happened had I blanched it before. The flavour was still amazing though and it felt great to make food from a weed.

Stickyweed Tea

Handful of stickyweed

Hot water

This is so simple to make and tastes very cleansing. I placed a handful of stickyweed in a teapot, poured on hot water and drank throughout the day. It helps to cleanse the lymphatic system and feels great for your body.

I have also made a stickyweed tincture consisting of apple cider vinegar and stickyweed. I have yet to try this for myself but when I do will update my blog.

Thyme

Thymus Vulgaris

Thyme is one of those herbs that I have had in my store cupboard since leaving home. I would shake some into my soups and stews but never really considered using it for anything else until this year. So many of these herbs have been used for eons, yet many of us have lost touch with them. The ease of buying our herbs from the supermarket has stopped many of us from truly connecting and growing our own herbs. I have always tried, where possible, to have something growing and, if you are limited for space, you can use window boxes or grow on windowsills. Anyway, I digress. Thyme was used by the Ancient Egyptians for embalming and the Greeks would burn it as an incense, believing it to be a herb of courage. The essential oil, thymol, is the main ingredient found in common mouthwashes sold in supermarkets.

Benefits

- Full of vitamin C to support our immune systems
- Can help with reducing inflammation in the body
- Can support healthy liver function
- Can help with respiratory conditions
- Can improve heart health
- Rich in Vitamin A which is great for helping with vision health

Uses

You can use this herb fresh in cooking or for making

teas. You can also dry it and use in the same way. I have mainly used this in teas but you can also rub it over your skin to keep mosquitoes at bay. Ideal in the summer months.

Dandelions

Taraxacum officinale

I love seeing these flowers pop up around the beginning of May. My guinea pigs are also huge fans of dandelion leaves! I remember when I was younger being told that if you picked them, you would wet the bed. The reason for this is that they act as a great diuretic. All parts of the dandelion plant can be eaten and are highly nutritious.

<u>Benefits</u>

- An excellent source of vitamins A,C and K
- The greens contain iron, calcium, magnesium and potassium
- The root can be dried and made into tea
- Full of antioxidants
- Can reduce inflammation
- Can lower blood pressure

- May promote liver health
- May have anti-cancer effects

Uses

I have used the dandelion leaves to make a pesto and pop into soups. The flowers can be made into syrups and salads. I have also used the leaves in tea when needing a bit of a detox.

Elderberry

Sambucus Nigra

I am so lucky to have an elder tree just outside my caravan. I was first introduced to elderberries a few years ago by a friend who took me foraging. We went off armed with an umbrella to reach the high branches. The berries kept landing on my head. She taught me how to make an elderberry syrup. I was so excited to make my first batch but massively underestimated the amount of berries I would need to make a litre of syrup. I spent four hours preparing my first batch to create 100ml! Since then, I have realised that I need a bit more than a handful. Full of antioxidants, these berries are amazing to help you get through the winter months and boost your immune system. We also have the beautiful flowers which appear around June time.

Benefits

- Antioxidant, anti-inflammatory and anti-bacterial
- Contains vitamin C and is great for boosting the immune system
- Contains tannins that create an astringent action and helps dry up runny eyes and noses
- Elderflowers can support the nervous system through stressful periods

Uses

The elderflowers themselves can be picked and used fresh or dried in a wardrobe. Please note that the leaves, twigs and roots are toxic. The berries are also toxic so please do not eat raw. They can be heated in a pan and strained through a muslin to make your syrup which you can keep in a fridge and have a tablespoon every morning.

Creating your own apothecary

As the NHS begins to crumble, more of us are looking at taking responsibility for our own health and wellbeing. I have begun to create my own apothecary using the herbs and plants around me and this may be something you also wish to create for yourself. You can dry your herbs in a dark place ready for the winter months. These are some of products that I have currently. Some are picked and dried and some have been bought:

- Nettle seeds, for teas and smoothies
- Nuts - almonds, cashews, walnuts
- Dates
- Chia seeds
- Dried fruit and peel
- Peppercorns
- Himalayan Salt
- Hibiscus flowers
- Hawthorn leaves
- Turmeric
- Bay leaves
- Oregano
- Thyme
- Mugwort
- Willow bark

- Rosemary

- Chives

What does the future hold?

As more and more of us begin to make the move, we will gradually come together in communities, some may set up accidentally, some may come together with more purpose and a vision, some may go from community to community learning skills, trading and bartering as we used to. For me, my vision is one of creating a healing centre with space for workshops and retreats that can be shared in the local community and for residents of the community. I want to have acres of land to which people can come to live and connect, not only to nature but also to reconnect to their inner knowing. I want a space where we can grow our own fruit and vegetables and, again, give back to the community in whatever form that may look like.

The idea of Temple Woman came to me whilst stomping in a field in the summer of 2021. 'What on earth is Temple Woman?', I thought to myself. Little did I know then what it would be. I sat down a couple of weeks later and wrote Temple Woman in big letters in the centre of a page and began to brainstorm - retreats, workshops, wellbeing days, online courses, a publishing house, mentoring, books, the idea being that a group would be formed as a community benefit society. We have an annual membership of £5 which goes back into the society. We have offerings where a percentage is put back into the society. The overall aim is to reconnect women to their inner knowing. If you read this and are male, don't worry there is room for you to join and support us too. Eventually, I would love a Temple Man but for now it is Temple Woman and one of our founding members has also come up with Temple Children. This has made me take another leap of faith, from my work as an individual to working as part of a group and co-creating something which will stand the test of time. A legacy.

Our publishing house is now set up and we are publishing books by women authors whose voices need to be heard, women who have stories to share but can't find a publisher or are having to search through the minefield of information around self-publishing. I know,

I've been there!

We want to raise money to create these offgrid communities that everybody so desires and is searching for; to be able to pay for land or structures or materials needed to fulfil our vision. Once costs for this book are covered, I will be donating a future percentage of my book earnings to the project. As members, we all have a say in how the society is run. Everyone has a voice.

Although I am not 100% sure where my journey will take me next, what I do know is that I have faith and trust that we will get to where we need to be. All of us. For those who have already taken the leap of faith, thank you. For those thinking of taking the leap, amazing. For those even mildly curious about doing it, keep researching it.

Chapter 8 - Channelings

7/2/2021

Where to be?

Who to be?

Those are the questions most asked

We know

We hear, we listen

We whisper back

You are exactly where you need to be

Right now

You are exactly who you need to be

In this moment

Stay. Be present. Allow. Accept

In the moment

Beat by beat

Are you present?

Are you there?

Are you in the moment?

Or elsewhere?

3/3/2021

Beyond

Beyond your perceptions and limitations

There lies

More

To be seen and experienced

Your idea of heaven will appear on Earth

Where the sun shines

Bountiful fruit will grow

Mother Earth will deliver

Her promise

That was made

To nurture and care for the citizens of Planet Earth

We rise as a collective

We evolve to the next stage

Lightness, enjoyment, abundance

Be present, aware

Open to the opportunities and abundance

Which come your way

11/04/2021

I have been here the whole time. Who? You. You are me and I am you. I feel you and you feel me. Our energies blend and merge and dance. Sometimes, you feel my emotions intensely and sometimes I feel yours. We are one. Our thoughts blend. We love unconditionally, yet our egos sometimes block and constrict the flow. Keep healing and working on yourself as I will on me. We are destined and neither of us can stop that. We have work to do which we will as we are both committed to being of service to others. We agreed before we came here to be of assistance and that we shall be.

My head is not in the clearest of spaces right now and there is stuff I know I need to sort out and change and that will happen. I've hurt every person I've ever been with and I don't want to do that to you which is why I have pulled away and detached. Deep down I know, and my heart knows, but I didn't feel ready to have all of these feelings for you. You have confused my mind and your power is quite intense. I need some time to chill and get my head in gear. Do know that I immensely value and appreciate you and our connection will always be there regardless of our distance or things I may say. You know it's my ego and I'm trying to control the situation around me as best I can as it makes me feel safe. I'll come back to you when I feel aligned and ready.

For now, be my friend, support me and trust me. I love you. I love you too.

17/4/2021

Listen more and speak less. You will find out more from words which aren't spoken than the words that are. Often people say what they think you want or need to hear rather than what is truly going on. Sometimes they don't know the words to say. Listen to their feelings. Tune into their energy. What are they not saying? This is the art of learning to really listen. The words are words but the feelings and emotions are true and speak louder than any words. Practise listening beyond words.

As the heart calls forth
The initial underlying pain
It opens the crevice
That has always been there

The pain flows out

Like molten lava

Trickling from the space

Where underneath the hurt and trauma

Lies the origin

Of pure love

Pure unconditional love

Which has always been there

Yet covered, suppressed, hidden

Chinks of light

Occasionally coming through

Yet it's taken time, maybe years to remember

Love comes from within

It lives within you

It is not something to earn

It cannot be owned

You do not have love

You are love

As love begins to pour from your heart

It touches others

They feel it

And it begins to open their hearts

Too

To their own place of unconditional love

Love is a practice

Practise every day

Loving you

Loving others

The vibration of love is so high

It negates any fear

How to show yourself love

How to show others love

Be kind. Listen. Be thankful.

Be kind. Listen. Be thankful.

We love you

22/5/2021

We adorn our homes with things that make us feel safe

We decorate it so

We may feel better

We plan and meticulate

How it can change

We constantly change the interior of our home

Yet

What if

This was merely a façade?

And by actually changing

Everything you could see

Didn't actually alter anything at all

Yet

By changing that which you can't see

You alter everything

Perception

What we perceive to be

Comfort and security

Is not

What we perceive to be

Home

Is not

Forget the external

And start within

For this is where you find

Home

Comfort

Security

And nowhere else

4/6/2021

No-one can ever leave you

In the sense you believe

There may be physical separation

However, energies are intertwined

Souls will always reconnect

And remember and recognise

We are at home within you

Do you hear us calling?

Our voices growing louder

For all to hear

And working with those

To also be voices for us

We are grateful for the assistance

You are all providing

At this time

Voices are getting louder

We are needed at this time

And necessary for the shift taking place

10/6/2021

Torn between the need to do and be

Striking a balance

Allowing and forcing

Creating and surrendering

Push, pull, push, pull

There is truly an art

To being

And it is only through

Practice

That we can attain it

As one practises to become an artist, musician or actor

One must also practise being

Still. Alone.

Without noise or distraction

Of busyness

Everything gets done when it is meant to

The art of being

Gives you space

To do in a more productive and orderly fashion

Doing without being

Brings chaos and disharmony

Being without doing

Creates indecision and stagnancy

When we have both

We have harmony and creation

Embrace the being

20/6/2021

Loving you

Loving others

The vibration of love is so high

It negates any fear

How to show yourself love

How to show others love

Be kind. Listen. Be thankful.

Be kind. Listen. Be thankful.

We love you x

What do I need to know today?

Calm, like a vast ocean on a sunny day

Allow the peace to begin within

And radiate out

To the world at large

Feeling frustration at the world

Means there is frustration within

Which needs to be tended and explored

Why are you angry with the world?

What did it do to you?

Are you angry with yourself?

If so, where?

Identify and pinpoint where the anger actually resides

In healing the anger within

You heal the anger without

22/6/2021

Channeled writing on Flat Earth

This is an interesting topic for discussion, Lindsay, and one which has been debated for eons. You may compare it to the Truman Show and you are not far off.

The weather is controlled. Every day, we ensure the sun rises and sets, the moon waxes and wanes. There are certain things which need to happen for the Earth to be in rhythm and cycles. The planets are not out there but within. Think of the movies like Lord of the Rings where there are different earths. Your land is flat and, yes, there are things underneath. As shamans have travelled to lower and upper worlds that is also what you have on Earth. With the naked eye, you cannot always see them and have massively tuned out.

Going forwards, this will change. For now, more are beginning to become aware, to feel multidimensional beings around them. Concepts and belief systems which have been embedded for years are coming to the surface to be destroyed and eliminated so we don't carry these forward to future generations. They may come as shocks to some of you, yourself included, but they will be overcome.

26/6/2021

Dear one

The time for resting will soon be over but for now it is an essential part of the cycle. Down time, rest, relax, rejuvenate. We have been working on your physical and energy bodies and you are now integrating these. You are being invited to eat fresh fruit and vegetables, to drink more water, to lighten your load. Do not feel guilty for this time dear one. As I have said, it is essential to rest right now. When you are in a space of joy and happiness, your energy vibrates at a higher frequency which affects not only you but all those around you and who you come into contact with. Keep doing the things which bring you joy - laugh, sing, dance, connect. Even though these sound like simple things, they have a big impact and this is the work, or part of the work, that you came here to do. Rest, relax, rejuvenate. We thank you for your time.

05/07/2021

To the men doing the work

We thank you

To the men who came before you and had no guidance

We thank you

To the men who stay still

And left

We thank you

To the men who fought

We thank you

To the men on their soul path

We thank you

To the men meditating

We thank you

And embracing their inner child

We thank you

To the men learning compassion

And empathy

We thank you

To the men speaking their truth

We thank you

To the men finding their inner strength

We thank you

To the men holding space for men and women

We thank you

To the men sharing their wisdom

We thank you

To the men sharing their truths

We thank you

To the men practising kindness and compassion

We thank you

To the men embracing their uniqueness

We thank you

To the men honouring all parts of themselves

We thank you

To the men willing to grow and expand

We thank you

To the men stepping forward

Into the Unknown

We thank you

To the men willing to not conform

We thank you

To the men I have had the pleasure to meet and to connect

with along my path

I thank you

07/07/2021

If Trees Could Talk

If trees could talk

What would they say?

Hello, how are you? Good day

I'm sure they would impart

More knowledge and wisdom than that

But what a pleasant start

The years they have stood

And seen and heard

Conversations over the years

Seasons coming and going

Braving all of the elements

And still standing strong

Unphased, unbending, unnerved

Whisperings occur between

The branches

Have you seen? Have you heard?

Connecting and talking

To each other

And to you

When trees talk

Listen and hear

To the wisdom they impart

18/7/2021

The channels are becoming clearer. Crown chakras are being felt and activated as we approach the 8th day of the 8th month. There is a time of heightened intuition for many. Gifts are being remembered such as telepathy and those who are meant to be guiding and leading will feel this pull. It will be made possible for land to become *available yet for many there is still work to do around the ego, the desire to control and profit from this. Yes, we understand that for now money is needed. However, in order to come together there must be ego dissolution and for communities to be run on a selfless basis. For them to be established for the greater good. It is not enough to declare that one wants to go offgrid and live with others in a space without doing the work they need on themselves. It is a constant evolution that the soul needs to purge and release and have a desire to live and work with others for the greater good. We have seen civilizations before grow then fall but this time is different. So many cycles. And now is the time for the civilization to proceed forward. There will be many scientists and builders and free energy as well as a need for spiritual mentors. Bring everyone in for everyone's skills are necessary. You all can learn from each other and teach each other. Learning to live together may not be an easy option yet it is the one that is needed to pave the way for the rest of humanity. Come together for the collective. There may be disagreements and arguments. Conflicts may arise. Yet these come about so you can learn new ways of communicating and handling these conflicts. There will be no 'one size fits all' in terms of how each community works yet there will be certain tools which will help and which can be put into place to allow all parties to communicate. Do not worry about the land, as it will come about.*

28/7/2021

A path of light

Illuminates the way

Through the door we must all head

Slowly, slowly we ascend

Stepping into the New Earth

Our new way of being and living

Rejoice

For it is already here

Every day one step forward

Every day changes within

And so, without

Carry on forward

30/7/2021

Our children chose us as their custodians on Earth.

We are their guides and mentors as they are ours.

Nurture them well for they are our future growers and builders.

Allow their creativity to pour forth without the limitations or beliefs that society places on them.

They are free beings and their souls, as ours, are ascending.

We have all chosen this time to be here.

Embrace it in the knowing you are a part of this.

This is a transformative time in history.

10/1/2022

I will not walk in front of you

But beside you

Through your pain and hurt

And darkness

I will be there

Holding a light in front

So we both may see

And tread

A little along the path

You do not need to see the full path

Or what lies at the end of the path

For now, all I ask of you

Is to trust

In yourself

That by placing one foot in front of another

That you will reach your destination

At times the darkness

May feel heavy and as if you are

Engulfed

Yet this is temporary

I cannot say exactly how long it may last

Yet I will say it is not permanent

Nor your permanent state

There is light within you

And if you cannot find it

We will send another

To help you find your own light

And in so doing

Later on your light will help another

1/2/2022

The times we talked about are in hand

When we saw into the future, we did not know the year

Or how long

Little did we know it would be several civilisations

Yet here you all are

And managing it

Just as we foresaw

Many of you were spirit guides to us

And now we return the favour

All is one

Connected

You are the change

The change to the civilisation as we know it

We saw it happening

As you are now

It is very exciting for us to watch

And we pray for you

As much as you pray too

Your purpose is so much bigger than you thought

Continue and have patience

As you say, Rome was not built in a day

Changes day by day

Support you in making a big change

For to make a big change feels huge

To make little changes feels not enough

Yet is

We love you

We see you

We support you

Conclusion

As I head towards the one-year anniversary of my offgrid journey, I not only wanted to share some of my journey with you but also some of the channelings that have come through in a year when many hoped that life would go 'back to normal'. I have also included some of the recipes I have used and made with the berries and plants I began to forage around the autumn time. As I have spent more time outdoors, I have felt more connected to myself and the Earth in ways I never have before. I am holding my vision strong for a wellbeing centre with space for community, being self-sustainable, honouring the cycles of the land and working with the Earth instead of against her. I know the land will appear when she is ready and it is not for me to force it but to know that, when it appears, the time will be right.

I am so grateful to be on this journey, to have met many amazing souls along the way, to be continually inspired by the work they are doing in creating and building new communities and spaces where we can live freely and fully in our sovereignty.

Now it is your turn... where will your offgrid adventure take you? I would love to hear your story

A Prayer for Humanity

At this time, I pray

I pray for all souls to awaken

I pray for our ancestors to come forth

And release us from their pain

For our pain is no longer their pain

I pray for our ancestors to encircle us

And be with us during this time

I pray that I may act always

From a space of love

And compassion

And empathy

I pray that the tides will turn

And no longer will we see

Poverty, hunger, homelessness

Abuse, addictions, hurt

I pray that we learn to live in love, to be love

I pray that every person on this planet finds peace in their heart

And their mind

I pray for our children

That they do not grow up into the system we became indoctrinated into

That our children will not have to work on their healing as much as we have

I pray that together we may unite against the tyranny of this world

That brothers and sisters will stand

Arm in arm

Shoulder to shoulder

Hand in hand

I pray that we find the strength within us

To stand up for ourselves

To stand up for what we know deep down to be right and true

I pray that we continue to find ways to connect across the miles

Sharing stories and experiences

I pray that we all find our place of peace

And in so doing, share it with others

X

From the Author

Thank you so much for reading my book, I hope you enjoyed it and, if you would like to stay connected, you can subscribe to my newsletter here. (Link also in Resources)

To connect with me and continue to follow my journey, you can find me at:

Instagram

http://www.instagram.com/lindsaybanks_templewoman

YouTube

http://www.youtube.com/Lindsaybanks

Facebook

http://www.facebook.com/groups/consciousnessarising

Website

http://www.lindsaybanks.uk

Resources

<u>ONLINE GROUPS</u>

Telegram - Offgrid Community Network UK
https://t.me/+dGRsYktPBblkOTRk

Facebook - Awakened Offgrid Communities
https://www.facebook.com/groups/320312689646295/

<u>BOOKS</u>

'A Gentle Hug for the Soul'; Providing comfort & reassurance in times of need
https://bit.ly/agentlehugforthesoul

'Awaken the Soul'
https://amzn.to/3gLFDlH

'Voices from the Past, Present & Future; Insights into 2020 and Beyond'
https://amzn.to/3FO5ab3

<u>NEWSLETTER</u>
https://mailchi.mp/dfe47b5df526/stay-in-touch

FREE GUIDE TO EARNING MONEY OFFGRID

https://templewoman.podia.com/free-guide-to-earning-money-offgrid

TEMPLE WOMAN ETSY STORE

https://www.etsy.com/uk/shop/TempleWoman

TEMPLE WOMAN PUBLISHING

http://www.templewomanpublishing.com

Temple Woman Publishing has been established to support aligned female authors in writing, editing, marketing and self-publishing their books.

You will find a warm welcome, a nurturing community of like-minded women and a home for your creative facility. It's a place of spirituality and freedom, of acceptance and understanding; a place to write, to create and to be your authentic self.

At Temple Woman Publishing, we want to enable our authors to focus on their writing and really enjoy the process without the pressure of deadlines or concerns about how to prepare, publish, market and sell their books.

We offer practical and spiritual support, an opportunity to be part of a community of like-minded authors who understand and encourage each other and, of course, we offer our joint expertise to help you to successfully publish your book. We are with you from the dreaded blank page, through emotional blockages and crises of confidence, to promoting your published book.

Do you want to write your own book?

If so and you want to self-publish, contact us at http://www.templewomanpublishing.com

Lindsay & June

Temple Woman Publishing

Printed in Great Britain
by Amazon

82949705R00081